Business and Technology (BT)

Diploma in business and technology

Pocket Notes

KAPLAN PUBLISHING

British library cataloguing-in-publication data

A catalogue record for this book is available from the British Library.

Published by:
Kaplan Publishing UK
179 - 191 Borough High Street
London
SE1 1HR

ISBN 978-1-83735-297-5

Printed and bound in Great Britain.

Contents

Structure of the examination

Format of the examination:

- Two hour computer based assessment

The exam will be made up of:

- Thirty 2-mark questions
- Sixteen 1-mark questions
- Six 4-mark questions
- Questions may be based around short scenarios four or five lines long

Core areas of the syllabus:

(A) Understand the purpose and types of business and how they interact with the key stakeholders and the external environment.

(B) Understand business organisation structure, functions and the role of corporate governance.

(C) Recognise the functions, systems and new technologies in accountancy and audit in communicating, reporting and assuring financial information, including the effective compliance, internal control and security of financial and other data.

(D) Recognise the principles of authority and leadership and how teams and individuals are recruited, managed, motivated and developed.

(E) Understand the importance of personal effectiveness as the basis for effective team and organisational behaviour.

(F) Recognise that all aspects of business and finance should be conducted in a manner which complies with and is in the spirit of accepted professional ethics and professional values.

All areas are equally weighted, so expect to see 8 or 9 questions in each area.

Keys to success

Your requirements:

- You are expected to demonstrate knowledge and understanding of the relevant theory.
- You are expected to assimilate idea, understand them and apply them to the "real world" situations.
- You must be able to recognise the needs for, and the differences between, procedures, processes and wider issues of management.

Preparation for the exam

- Questions may combine or integrate more than one topic area, so revise thoroughly.
- All topics are equally important, make sure you have covered the entire syllabus. A shallow but broad knowledge is required rather than focussing on just a few areas.
- Read the question requirement carefully before selecting an answer.
- Answer all questions, this will maximise your chances of passing the exam.

Quality and accuracy are of the utmost importance to us so if you spot an error in any of our products, please send an email to mykaplanreporting@kaplan.com with full details, or follow the link to the feedback form in MyKaplan.

Our Quality Co-ordinator will work with our technical team to verify the error and take action to ensure it is corrected in future editions.

chapter

1

Business organisation, its structure and culture

In this chapter

- The need for organisation and its types.
- Different structural types.
- Boundaryless organisations.
- Planning levels – The Anthony Triangle.
- The roles of main organisational functions and co-ordinating mechanisms between them.
- Marketing.
- Organisational culture.
- The impact of the informal organisation.

Exam focus

- You need to gain a general understanding of what types of organisations there are and how the activities of different departments are aligned.
- Be aware of the links between organisational structure and culture. Some structures encourage a certain cultural stance, e.g. functional structure and role culture.

The need for organisation and its types

Organisations are social arrangements for the controlled performance of collective goals

- Two or more people working together in a structured way Duties and responsibilities being asigned to each individual
- Organisations use systems (e.g. swiping in when entering office) and procedures (e.g. cash handling rules) to regulate staff behaviour
- All organisations pursue certain goals, these are considered to be over and above indivdual aspirations

Organisations exist:

- to satisfy social needs
- to overcome the individuals' limitations
- to enable individuals to specialise
- to save time through joint effort
- to pool knowledge and ideas
- to pool expertise
- to provide synergy.

Organisational types

Organisations can differ depending on their areas of activity, geographical spread of operations, size etc. However the two main types of the organisation can be classified:

1 by profit orientation

- profit-seeking organisations:
  seek to maximise the wealth of their owners
  (e.g. commercial companies)
- not-for-profit organisations (NFPs):
  seek to satisfy the needs of their members, profit is no longer a primary objective
  (e.g. schools, hospitals).

2 by ownership/control

- public sector:

  provision of basic governmental services
  (e.g. police, education, healthcare)
- private sector limited liability (Ltds and plcs)
  - partnerships
  - clubs
- cooperatives owned by people who buy or use their services.

Different structural types

Definition

Structure refers to the way jobs are grouped into different departments and are allocated responsibility and authority.

Type	Rationale
Entrepreneurial	Typical in small, owner-managed companies. Allows for fast decision-making and high degree of control, however may restrict growth and success depends on manager's capabilities.
Functional	Departments are based on common specialisation. Best suited to companies operating in a stable environment, dealing with few products, this structure often suffers from conflict between departments and slow decision-making.
Divisional	Functions are grouped in accordance with product lines or divisions. Gives more responsibility to general managers, allows senior staff to become more strategic, but functions are duplicated and divisions may lose sight of organisation-wide goals.
Geographical	Activities are grouped according to location. This gives a high degree of flexibility necessary to adjust for local customs, but may lead to sub-optimisation.
Matrix	A combination of functional and divisional structure which allows for better coordination of activities and more focus on operations. Can lead to dual reporting and excessive pressure on staff.

Boundaryless Organisations

Definition

Boundaryless organisations are a modern model of organisational design which adopt a flexible, unstructured design.

Type	Rationale
Hollow organisations	All non-core (i.e. non-strategically important) functions are outsourced to third party organisations.
Virtual organisations	Any, and all, functions can be outsourced – whether core or non-core. All that is left is a small central staff who co-ordinate the outsourcing arrangements.
Modular organisations	Boundaryless manufacturing organisations. Rather than simply making their own product, they break the manufacturing process down into modules or components. Each component can then be either made by the company or outsourced.

Definition

Scalar chain – number of management levels

Span of control – number of subordinates under one manager's control

Span of control depends on:

- managers capabilities (physical & mental limitations)
- nature of managers workload
- nature of work undertaken (how routine it is)
- geographical dispersion of subordinates
- level of cohesiveness within the team.

All structures could be divided into two groups

- By composition (in relation to its size)
  - Tall with many levels of hierarchy & narrow span of control (e.g. functional, divisional, geographic)
  - Flat with few levels of hierarchy & wide span of control (e.g entrepreneurial, matrix).
- By level of decision-making:
  - Centralised – decisions are made by senior management (e.g.functional, entrepreneurial).
  - Decentralised – decision-making is delegated to lower levels (e.g.matrix, geographical).

Offshoring

This refers to the process of outsourcing or relocating some of an organisation's functions from one country to another, usually in an effort to reduce costs.

Shared services approach

This involves centralising an internal function that is currently used throughout the organisation (i.e. centralisation of the IT department) and then running it like a separate business within the organisation. This often means that the rest of the organisation will be charged for use of this function.

Planning levels – The Anthony Triangle

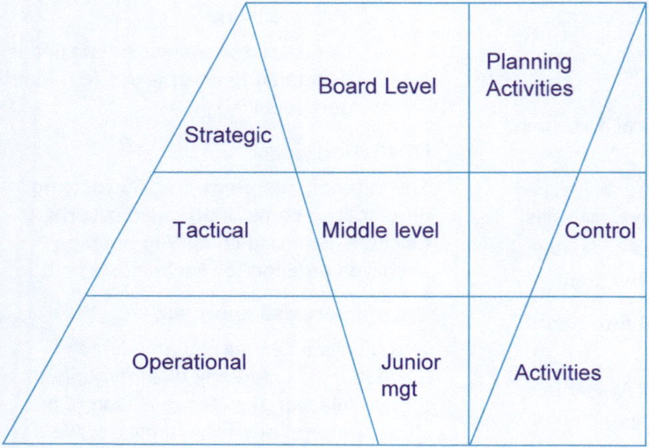

- long term
- looks at the whole organisation
- defines resource requirements

- medium term
- looks at the department / divisional level
- specifies how to use resources

- short term
- very detailed
- concerned day-to-day running of the company

Definition

Strategy is a course of action, including the specification of resources required, to achieve a specific objective.

Levels of strategy

Corporate – directions for the whole of the organisation.

Business – how to approach a particular market.

Operational – specific to each department.

The roles of main organisational functions and co-ordinating mechanisms between them

Departments and their roles

- R&D – developing & improving products
- Purchasing – acquiring input materials, negotiating trading terms (e.g. quantity quality, price)
- Production – converting supplies into finished goods, adding value in the process
- Marketing – product design, pricing, distribution, promotion (4Ps of marketing mix)
- Services – customer services, dealing with complaints and enquiries
- Admin – back-office, supporting functions
- Finance – financial reporting, treasury, management accounting
- HR- dealing with staff issues

Coordination through:

- Standardised: Work processes (aiming for single best practice), Output (developing product/service specifications), Skills and knowledge (staff training)
- Direct supervision (managerial oversight)
- Mutual adjustment (via communication)

Marketing

Definition

Marketing is a management process that identifies, anticipates and satisfies customer needs efficiently and profitably.

The organisation could have different attitudes towards customers:

- product orientation: producing goods of optimum quality in hope they will be bought
- sales orientation: using aggressive sales techniques to persuade people to buy
- marketing orientation: putting customer at the centre of organisational activity and ensuring the product satisfies their needs.

Marketing mix allows the balance of organisational capacity and customer requirements and includes:

- product (e.g. design, features, packaging)
- price (e.g. discounts, credit policy, payment terms)
- promotion (e.g. advertising, personal selling, direct marketing)
- place (e.g. distribution channels, transportation, warehousing).

In the service sector marketing mix is extended to include:

- people (e.g. employee selection, training and motivation)
- physical evidence (e.g. layout, décor, presentation)
- process management (e.g. customer handling from the first to the last contact).

Organisational culture

- A set of norms of behaviour
- Formal rules (e.g. employment contract terms)
- Informal rules (e.g. tea breaks)

Symbols and symbolic actions

- Rituals (e.g. celebrations)
- Logos
- Slogans
- Badges

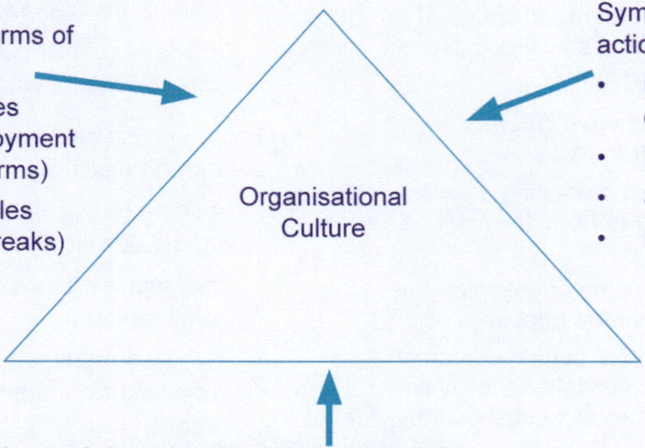

A set of shared values/dominant beliefs

- Underlying attitudes (e.g. to work, customers, mistakes)
- Beliefs (e.g. importance of people as individuals)

Organisational culture depends on:

- size – turnover, physical size, employee numbers
- technology – attitudes to innovation, adoption of new working methods
- diversity – product range, geographical spread, cultural make-up of stakeholders
- age – years in business, depth of managers' experience
- history – what has worked in the past, previous successes and failures
- ownership – number and type of shareholders.

Schein argued that the first leaders of an organisation create its culture and described three levels of culture:

- artifacts – can be easily seen (e.g. office layout and environment, dress code)
- espoused values – play a supporting role in bringing people together (e.g. slogans)
- basic assumptions – difficult to identify, work at unconscious level (e.g. respect for management instructions).

Handy defined corporate culture as "the way we do things around here".

He identified the following four cultural types:

Power • Found in smaller, entrepreneurial organisations • One major source of influence (e.g. founder) • Few formal rules	**Task** • Project-based, creative work • Nothing is allowed to get in the way of achieving the goals • Suitable in a rapidly changing environment
Role • Common in bureaucratic organisations (e.g. government) • People follow predetermined procedures without questioning their purpose • Emphasis on the individual's position in the hierarchy	**Person** • Serves the interest of the individuals who make it up (e.g. solicitors firm) • Is built around educated and articulate individuals – specialists with a common interest • Success of the organization depends on retaining the key personnel

Hofstede attempted to identify how national culture influences business behaviour:

Trait	**High**	**Low**
Individualism (vs. collectivism) – tendency for people to look after themselves and their immediate families	Staff expect to be assessed on their own merits	Staff expect to be assessed as groups
Uncertainty avoidance (UA index) – extent to which people dislike risk	Staff expect to be given detailed guidelines and rules	Staff like taking their own initiative
Power Distance (PD) – extent to which inequality in power is accepted	Managers are expected to be powerful	Staff expect to be involved in decision-making
Motivation towards achievement and sucess	Motivation by job titles, increased status and pay rises	Motivation by work-life balance, quality of life and relationships at work
Long-term orientation (vs. short term orientation)	Long term – focus is on future rewards, saving, persistence and ability to adapt	Short-term – focus on respect for tradition, social obligations and 'saving face'
Indulgence vs. restraint	Indulgence – focus on enjoying life and having fun	Restraint – strict social norms

The impact of the informal organisation

In the organisation people often socialise across divisional boundaries. This is referred to as the **informal organisation** – it is a flexible arrangement with fluctuating membership.

Features of the informal organisation.

- People are joined by a common interest (network of relationships based on friendship).
- A separate set of procedures (people doing favours for each other).
- Grapevine communication network (circulating gossips and rumours).

Impact of the informal organisation

Positive

- Can be used by management to complement the existing structure and strengthen the bonds between staff.
- Things can get done quicker.
- Monitoring the grapevine allows to resolve problems before they escalate.

Negative

- Being part of the informal organisation means that manager loses his/her impartial standing and becomes emotionally involved with staff.
- "Cutting corners" exposes the organisation to additional risks e.g. safety failures.

chapter

2

Information technology

In this chapter

- Information and data.
- Computerisation.
- Types of information systems.
- Financial technology.

Exam focus

- Make sure you understand the difference between data and information and how the latter is used in business organisations.
- You need to understand the main features of the five information systems and how they aid management's work.
- You need to understand the impact that financial technology has on business and the accounting profession. (Namely, cloud computing, artificial intelligence, blockchain technology, big data and cyber security).

Information and data

Exam focus

Data is a collection of symbols, raw facts and transactions that have been recorded but not yet processed. It could be

- quantitative – capable of being measured numerically
- qualitative- subjective, may reflect distinguishing characteristics.

Information is data that has been processed in such a way that it becomes meaningful.

Information requirements:

By management	By third parties
• For recordkeeping and analysis • Planning and controlling • Serves as a basis for decision-making • Necessary to monitor and evaluate progress towards achieving goals	• By owners to assess the performance of the company • By suppliers as a pre-requisite for trade negotiations • By employees to find out about their work results • By law companies are obliged to submit certain information to tax authorities

Qualities of good information

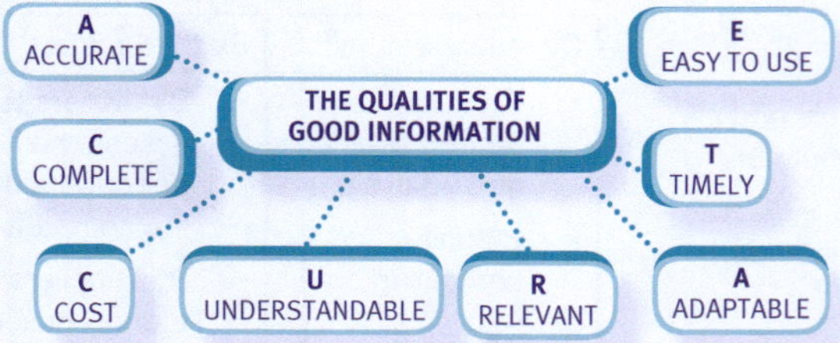

Information for decision-making

Strategic level	• Used to plan long-term strategy • Mainly from external sources • Usually in summarized form and on an ad-hoc basis
Tactical Level	• Instructions from the strategic level • Regular quantitative reports from the operational level • Summarised form with further details attached
Operational level	• Information and instructions from the tactical level • Primarily concerned with day-to-day performance • Information from internal sources – detailed and precise

Computerisation

Computer technology includes:

- intranet (can only be accessed by organisational members)
- extranet (access is granted to authorised third parties e.g. suppliers)
- database (shared facility for storing large amounts of data)
- spreadsheet (tool designed to analyse data)

	Advantages	Disadvantages
Database	Avoids duplication Ease of reporting and sharing data Consistency of input data	Enhanced security due to restricted access High level of skill is required to use it Requires a greater initial financial investment System failures could be widespread
Spreadsheet	Easy to use Familiar to most computer operators Allows the user to manipulate the data in variety of ways	A lot of copying and pasting is done manually Sharing information is difficult Size and volume restrictions
Accountancy packages	Rapid recording of transactions vs. manual system Less chance of mistakes Rapid production of reports and financial statements	Usually requires training Can be expensive May be unnecessary for a low level of transactions

Types of information systems

1 Transaction processing system (TPS) (e.g. Payroll):

- looks at individual transactions
- routine reporting
- used by junior management
- concerned with recording and basic processing.

2 Management information system (MIS) (e.g. simple database application):

- converts data from TPS into information
- used by middle management
- generates ad-hoc reports
- concerned with monitoring performance and coordination.

3 Executive information system (EIS) (e.g. complex database application):

- concerned with monitoring business results and general business conditions
- flexibility in data reporting, including drill-down facility
- includes data from internal and external sources
- used by senior management.

4 Decision support system (DSS) (e.g. modelling tool):

- requires significant expertise to use
- performs "what-if" analysis
- supports semi-structured and unstructured decisions
- includes statistical instruments.

5 Expert system (e.g. bank loan approval):

- contains a knowledge database
- can be used at any management level
- relies on a set of rules to solve a problem
- can be used to automate manual processes.

Financial Technology

Cloud computing

Cloud computing is computing based on the internet. It avoids the need for software, applications, servers and services stored on physical computers. Instead, it stores these with cloud services providers who store these things on the internet and grant access to authorised users.

Benefits:

- Storing and sharing data
- On demand self-service
- Flexibility
- Collaboration
- More competitive
- Easier scaling
- Reduced maintenance
- Back ups and disaster recovery
- Better security

Artificial intelligence (AI)

Artificial intelligence is an area of computer science that emphasises the creation of intelligent machines that work and react like human beings.

- Machine learning algorithms detect patterns and learn how to make predictions and recommendations by processing data and experiences, rather than by explicit programming instruction.

Examples of how AI can be used in accountancy:

- Using maching learning to code accounting entries enabling greater automation
- Improving fraud detection through more sophisticated machine learning models
- Using machine learning – based predictive models to forecast revenues
- Improving access to and analysis of unstructured data.

Big data

Big data is a term for a collection of data which is so large that it becomes difficult to store and process using traditional databases and data processing applications.

Features of big data

According to Gartner, big data can be described using the '3Vs':

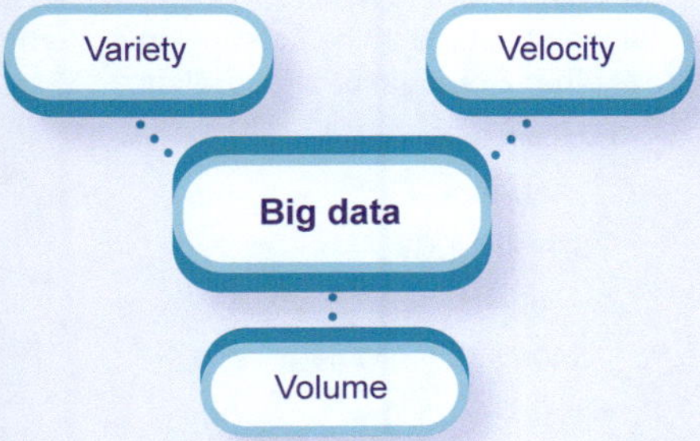

Another V which is sometimes added by organisations to the above list is:

- Veracity (truthfulness)

Benefits to the organisation:

- Driving innovation
- Gaining competitive advantage
- Improving productivity

Improving the effectiveness of accounting and audit:

Management accounting	Big data will contribute to the development of effective internal control systems and budgeting processes.
Financial accounting	Big data will improve the quality and relevance of accounting information.
Reporting	Big data can assist with the creation and improvement of accounting standards.
Audit	Big data can enhance the quality and relevance of the audit through data analysis. It may be possible to test entire populations of audit-relevant data and provide more relevant business insights.

Blockchain technology

A blockchain has been described as a decentralised, distributed and public digital ledger that is used to record transactions across many computers so that the record cannot be altered retroactively without the alteration of all subsequent blocks and the consensus of the network.

Benefits of a blockchain:

- The main benefit of a blockchain is security.

A blockchain provides an effective control mechanism aimed at addressing cyber security risks.

Relevance of blockchain technology to accountants:

- Reducing the costs of maintaining and reconciling ledgers
- Providing certainty over the ownership and history of assets
- Helping accountants gain clarity over available resources
- Freeing up resources to concentrate on planning and valuation, rather that record-keeping.

Cyber security

Cyber security is the protection of internet – connected systems, including hardware, software and data, from cyber attacks.

A cyber attack is a malicious and deliberate attempt to breach the information system of another individual or organisation.

Key risks to data:

- Malware
- Phishing
- Denial of service attacks
- Man in the middle attacks

Protection of IT systems and software

Potential threat	**Solution**
Natural disasters e.g. fire, flood	• Fire procedures • Location e.g. not prone to floods • Back up procedures
Malfunction of hardware or software	• Network design • Back up procedures
Viruses	• Virus software • Formal security policy and procedures • Checks for unauthorised software
Hackers	• Firewall software • Passwords and usernames
Human errors	• Training

chapter

3

Environmental analysis

In this chapter

- Stakeholders.
- Political factors.
- Legal factors.
- Economic factors.
- Macroeconomics.
- Social factors.
- Technological factors.
- Competition.
- Porter's value chain.

Stakeholders

Exam focus

A stakeholder is a group or individual who has an affect on or is affected by the organisation.

Groups of stakeholders:

Group	Stakeholder	Expectations
Internal (parties inside the company)	Employees Directors	Jobs/careers Money/ benefits
Connected (have a contractual relationship with the company)	Shareholders Customers Financiers	Increase in wealth Value-for-money goods To repay the loan
External (outside the company with no contractual relationship)	Government General public Pressure groups	Jobs, taxes Considerate behaviour Reduce pollution

Stakeholders may also be classified as:

- Primary – those with a formal contractual relationship with the organisation, such as employees or shareholders.
- Secondary – those with an interest, but no formal contractual relationship with the organisation, such as the public or pressure groups.

Stakeholder conflict arises due to different nature of their interest (e.g. paying higher wages reduces profit and may create conflict between employees and shareholders).

Mendelow suggested using stakeholder mapping approach to identify and therefore try to satisfy the needs to most dominant stakeholders.

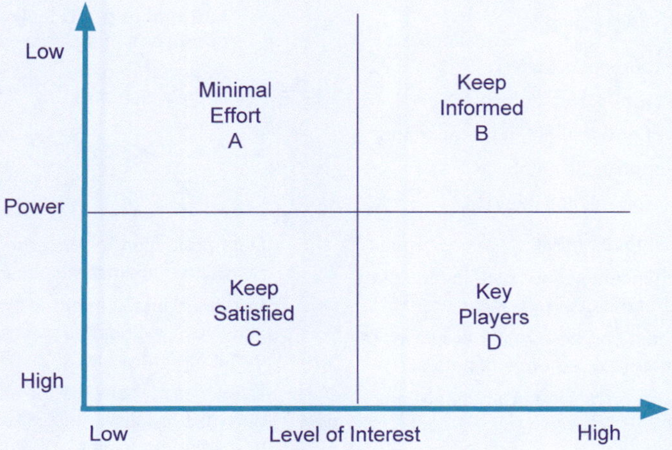

Exam focus

In the exam you will need to assess external environmental factors and consider their impact on an organisation.

Political factors

Political environment includes:

- political system and ideology
- the role of government in the economy
- the risk of political instability
- foreign trade relationships.

Impact of the government:

- providing incentives for certain industries in the form of subsidies or tax breaks
- government can be a major employer of a customer (e.g. defence contracts)
- decides on privatising or nationalising industries
- can discourage or attract foreign trade (eg. by using quotas, tariffs)
- is responsible for country's infrastructure (e.g. roads).

Levels of political system:

- **supra-national** (e.g. WTO promotes free trade and resolves trade disputes)
- **national** (e.g. EU looks after the operations of a single European market)
- **regional** (e.g. councils look after affairs in their district).

Legal factors

Exam focus

Data protection is concerned with protecting individuals against misuse of information.

Personal data is information about a living individual, including expressions of opinion about the individual.

Everyone responsible for using personal data has to follow strict rules called 'data protection principles'. The General Data Protection Regulation (GDPR) is an EU law introduced in 2018 which aims to make sure the information is:

1 used fairly, lawfully and transparently
2 used for specified, explicit purposes
3 used in a way that is adequate, relevant and limited to only what is necessary
4 accurate and, where necessary, kept up to date
5 kept for no longer than is necessary
6 handled in a way that ensures appropriate security, including protection against unlawful or unauthorised processing, access, loss, destruction or damage
7 A data user is responsible for the security and protection of data against unauthorised access, alteration, destruction, disclosure or accidental loss
8 Personal data should not be transferred to another country outside the European Economic Area unless that country ensures an adequate level of protection for the rights and freedoms of data subjects in relation to the processing of personal data.

The Data Protection Act 2018 supplements the GDPR and incorporates it into UK law.

There is strong legal protection for sensitive information, such as:

- race, ethnic background, religious beliefs
- political opinions
- trade union memberships
- genetics, biometrics (where used for identification), health
- sex life or orientation.

The need for consent underpins the principles. Individuals must opt-in whenever data is collected and there must be clear privacy notices. Those notices must be concise and transparent and consent must be able to be withdrawn at any time.

Economic factors

Exam focus

The examiner has indicated that many students are weak on economics. Ensure you understand the different objectives, problems, policies and solutions.

Exam focus

Microeconomics is the study of the economic behaviour of individual consumers, firms, and industries.

Macroeconomics considers aggregate behaviour, and the study of the sum of individual economic decisions.

Macroeconomics

Macroeconomics focuses on:

- overall "aggregate" demand for good and services
- output of goods and services (national product)
- supply of factors of production (labour, land, capital, entrepreneurship)
- total income earned by providers of factors of production
- money spent in purchasing national product (national expenditure)
- government policy.

Macroeconomic policy objectives:

- rising economic growth (increasing national income)
- low inflation
- full employment
- balanced balance of payments (difference between value of exports and imports).

Factors affecting the level of business activity:

- confidence of consumers and businesses in political stability and economic development
- aggregate demand: AD = C + I + G + X – M
  - consumer spending (C)
  - investment by firms (I)
  - government spending (G)
  - demand from exports (X)
  - demand for imports (M)
- capital, its availability and level of interest rates
- use of resources such as new technology, efficient working practices
- government policy on spending and taxation
- exchange rate movements, strength of the currency.

Definition

Trade cycle is a series of fluctuations in the rate of growth of real (inflation-adjusted) GDP over its long-run trend.

Recession	Falling demand, companies scale down output, unemployment rises, household consumption decreases
Slump/ depression	Low business confidence, heavy unemployment, low aggregate demand
Recovery	Could be due to new technology, economy picks up, demand increases, firms start to invest, reduction in unemployment, rising incomes
Boom	Economy is reaching it full capacity, shortages are possible, these are met by increase in prices rather than production

The role of the government is to smooth out this pattern and avoid "boom and bust" years.

Definition

Economic growth – arises from an increase in the quantity and/or quality of the factors of production in the economy.

Advantages	Disadvantages
Higher income per head	Depletion of natural resources
More jobs are available	Environmental pollution
Better standards of living	Saving to invest reduces consumption

Factors influencing growth.

- Volume of investment.
- Technological advancements.
- Increase in labour supply.
- Rise in international trade.
- Discovery of natural resources.

Policies to promote growth.

- Cutting interest rates.
- Running a budget deficit.
- Development grants and tax breaks for investors.
- Creating a stable economy.
- Reducing imports (e.g. protectionist measures).

Inflation

Definition

Inflation is a sustained increase in the general level of prices – a situation where average prices are rising over time. It leads to a fall in the purchasing power of money and an increase in the cost of living.

Deflation is a period of negative inflation.

Inflationary gap – increase in demand leads to increase in prices as resources are fully employed.

Deflationary gap – resources are underutilised, so any change of demand will affect output. Though prices are constant, the national income is below the full employment gap.

Stagflation – combination of high inflation and high unemployment.

Effects of inflation.

- Investment may be discouraged.
- Adverse balance of payments effects (expensive exports due to high inflation).
- Misallocation of resources thus decreasing economic growth.
- Social unrest due to uneven redistribution on wealth.
- Erosion in the real value of savings.
- Reduces the real value of a debt.
- Redistributes funds from taxpayers to the government in a progressive tax system.

Causes of inflation:	Possible solutions
• Demand pull – caused by excess AD 'too much money chasing too few goods'.	• Reduce AD – e.g. tax rises, cut in Government spending, increase in interest rates.
• Cost push – caused by rising production costs, especially labour costs. The initial cause of cost push inflation could be: – internal (e.g. pressure for rising living standards from powerful trade unions) – external (e.g. rising import prices, caused by a significant currency devaluation).	• Get agreement from trade unions not to demand higher wages (usually done as part of a "prices and incomes policy" where firms are also asked not to increase prices) • Take steps to strengthen domestic currency.
• Imported – caused by heavy reliance on imports and weak national currency.	• Encourage firms to use domestic products instead • Stengthen currency.
• Monetary – overexpansion in money supply.	• Restrict growth in money supply – e.g. print fewer notes, increase interest rates.
• Expectations (e.g. anticipation of rising prices leads people to demand higher wages) .	• Prices and income policy.

Unemployment

Is calculated as a percentage of unemployed compared to total workforce.

Problems of unemployment.

- To pay benefits to unemployed government has to increase taxes.
- Is often linked to crime, poor health, family breakdown.
- Restricts economic growth.
- Unemployed will gradually lose their skills.
- Increases income inequality.

Categories of unemployment.

- Frictional: due to people changing their jobs, normally only short term.
- Seasonal: related to predictable cycles in demand (e.g. tourism).
- Real wage: power of unions keeps the wages artificially high reducing number of jobs.
- Cyclical: caused mainly by insufficient demand and related to the trade cycle.
- Structural: caused by structural economic change (e.g. decline in manufacturing).
- Technological: a type of structural unemployment caused by industry moving towards more capital intensive and computerised methods.

To address the effect of unemployment government can:

- fund retraining schemes
- improve information on job vacancies
- provide aids and grants for industry relocation and redevelopment
- provide business start-up advice and initial loans
- encourage labour mobility
- deregulate the labour market.

Balance of payments

Definition

Balance of payment records all the transactions between residents of the country and overseas residents during a year.

Balance of payment is subdivided into three parts.

- Current account
  - the balance of trade in goods is often referred to as a 'balance of trade'. It is the value in pounds sterling of goods exported less goods imported.
  - the balance of trade in services is referred to as the 'invisible balance'.
- Capital account includes transfers of capital by government, or in foreign aid by businesses, and by individuals (e.g. migrant workers).
- Financial account records flows of capital, both short- and long-term investment.

Balance of payments deficit results from:

- excessive growth in aggregate monetary demand
- an overvalued exchange rate
- high domestic inflation
- depressed export markets, and falling export prices
- significant increases in the prices of essential imports.

Consequences of balance of payment deficit	Ways to rectify the situation
• Dependence on borrowing from abroad • Government has to sell more of its assets • Leads to devaluation of currency	• Expenditure-reducing strategies (e.g. reducing domestic demand through contractionary fiscal or monetary policy) • Expenditure-switching policy (e.g. encouraging expenditure on domestic products rather than imported goods)

Fiscal economic policy

Definition

Fiscal policies are concerned with government spending and taxation, and therefore government borrowing.

A government has a budget deficit when government spending exceeds taxation. There is a budget surplus when government spending is less than taxation. A balanced budget implies government spending approximately equals taxation.

Fiscal policy helps to smooth out cyclical fluctuations in aggregate monetary demand and is referred to as an 'automatic cyclical stabiliser'.

Budget deficit	Budget surplus
• Financed through borrowing • Helps to close the deflatory gap (e.g.by providing employment opportunities) • Is often referred to as "expansionary" policy as it boosts aggregate demand	• Is financed by taxation or printing more money • Used to deal with inflationary gap (e.g. by taking money out of the economy) • Is known as "contractionary policy"

Monetary policy

Definition

Monetary policy is the manipulation of the money supply, rate of interest, exchange rates or credit controls.

Targets of the monetary policy.

- Money supply – is a total supply of money in the economy including cash and bank deposits. This could be manipulated by requiring banks to keep a higher percentage of deposits in cash.
- Interest rates – are the price of money. Rise in rates makes investment less attractive.
- Exchange rates – fall in the rate will stimulate exports.
- Credit controls – restrictions on bank lending to reduce demand.

Theories on how to manage the economy

Classical view – do nothing.

- Government does not interfere.
- Economy will automatically move to equilibrium with full employment.
- During depression entrepreneurs will obtain factors of production cheaper.
- At the peak inflation is possible.

Demand side (Keynesian view).

- There is more than one equilibrium of supply/demand.
- Government need to intervene to move to a better equilibrium quicker.
- Governmental spending will stimulate economic growth.
- Money is then repaid through increase in future tax revenue.

Supply side (Friedman' monetarist view).

- Equilibrium will occur when supply is equal to demand in all markets of economy.
- Economy will naturally gravitate to the equilibrium unless hindered by market imperfections such as
  - inflation
  - government spending and taxation
  - minimum wages
  - regulation of markets.
- Role of government is to remove these imperfections.

Supply and demand

This looks at how supply and demand for goods and services vary with price.

The three graphs you should be aware of are:

The supply curve:

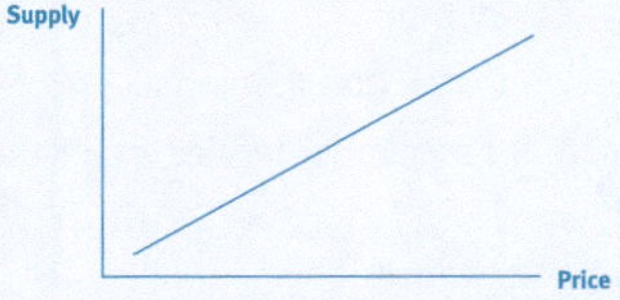

A shift in the supply curve can be caused by:

- Technological innovations
- Changes in production efficiency
- Input price changes
- Indirect taxes

The demand curve:

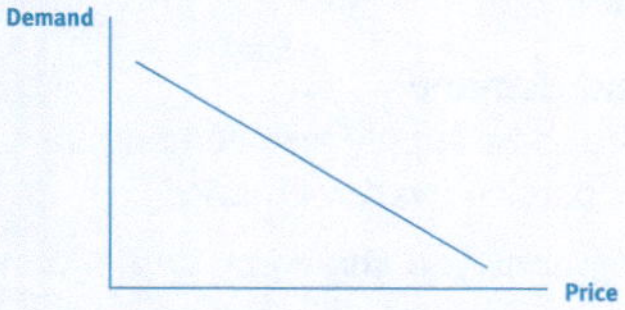

A shift in the demand curve can be caused by:

- Changes in income
- Changes in tastes and fashions
- The price of complementary or substitute goods
- Population changes

And the point they reach equilibrium:

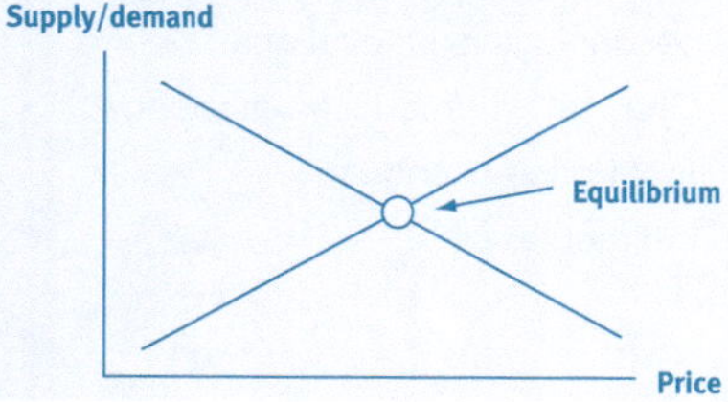

Price elasticity of demand (PED)

This looks at how far the number of units demanded by consumers will change as the price of the goods or services changes.

It is measured as:

$$\frac{\text{percentage change in quantity demanded}}{\text{percentage change in price}}$$

If the PED > 1, the product is described as elastic. If the PED < 1, the product is described as inelastic.

PED can be affected by a number of factors, including:

- The availability of substitutes
- The proportion of income spent on the product or service
- Whether the item is a necessity
- The duration of the change in price
- The definition of the market

Cost behaviour over time

Short term cost behaviour follows the **law of diminishing returns**, due to increasing inefficiency.

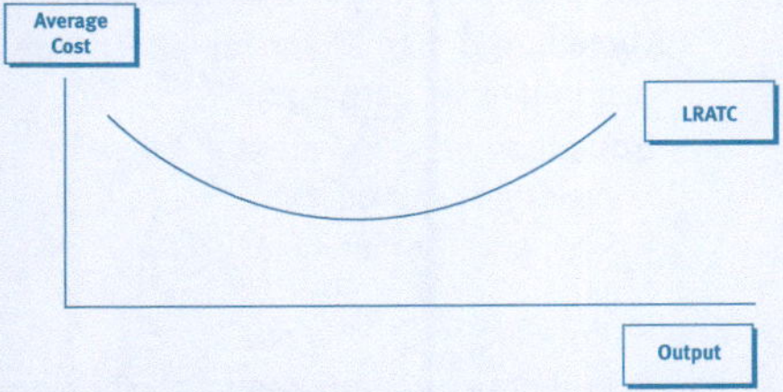

Long term cost behaviour follows a similar pattern due to increasing diseconomies of scale.

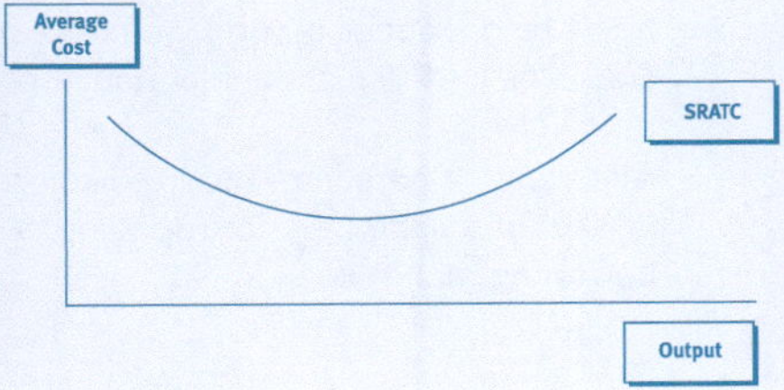

Perfect and imperfect markets

A perfect market exists when:

- There are large numbers of customers and suppliers
- The products sold by suppliers are identical
- There is perfect information
- There are no barriers to entry to, or exit from, the market.

Any market that does not conform to this is **imperfect**. Different types of imperfect market exist, depending on the level of competition within the market.

Definition

Competition refers to the rivalry amongst sellers as they try to increase their profits, sales volume or market share by varying their marketing mix (such as price, product, promotion or place).

Definition

Monopoly

This occurs when on company controls all, or nearly all, of the market for a particular product or service and therefore has little competition from rivals.

Monpolistic competition

This type of market occurs when a business has many different competitors, but each offers a somewhat differentiated product. For example, restaurants exist in such a market. Each restaurant is trying to attract the same customers, but each one offers different menu options cooked in a different way.

Oligopoly

Oligopolies are another form of imperfect market where the market is controlled by a small number of organisations. While there is no precise number typically the market must be dominated by between two and six different firms for it to be classed as an oligopoly.

Social factors

Key social and demographic issues.

- Population (e.g. birth rate and growth, composition by age, urbanisation).
- Wealth (e.g. high disposable income, distribution of earnings).
- Education (e.g. skilled staff thrive in knowledge economy).
- Health (e.g. obesity, HIV).

Cultural trends.

- Social structure – linked to social class – a group of people with the same social, economic or educational status.
- Values – the accepted behaviour that helps bind a social group together (e.g. concerns for the planet, importance of the family).
- Attitudes – a person or group's like or dislike for a thing (e.g. for recycling or borrowing money).

- Tastes – an individual's personal preferences and patterns of choice (e.g. fashion).

Governmental policy.

- Population (e.g. regulating birth rate via subsidies and penalties, raising retirement age).
- Housing (e.g. affordable homes for social workers).
- Employment (e.g. childcare provisions for single-parent families).
- Health (e.g. ban on smoking in public places).

Environmental issues

A business can affect the environment through:

- Pollution
- Consumption of resources
- Destruction of natural habitats

Don't forget that the environment can also impact on businesses:

- Climate and other environmental changes
- Lack of resources
- Polluting companies may damage their reputation
- Government legislation to protect the environment

Companies can try to minimise their impact on the environment by:

- Redesigning products to use fewer raw materials
- Reducing packaging
- Recycling
- Improving energy efficiency
- Careful production planning to reduce wastage

Ultimately, businesses should attempt to be **sustainable**, which involves using resources in such a way that the **needs of future generations are not compromised.**

Technological factors

Impact of technology.

- On organisational structure (e.g. downsizing, delayering, outsourcing).
- On products (e.g. sophisticated features, TV over broadband).
- On production processes (e.g. automation, better scheduling).
- On society (e.g. e-commerce, homeworking).

Benefits of technology for the organisation	Drawbacks of new technology
Staff are never out of touch (e.g. smartphones) Better work/life balance for staff (e.g. homeworking) Reduction in routine operations Efficient communication Easy to store and share digital information Outsourcing non-core functions	People often feel stressed or overloaded Lack of control over the volume of work done, need to purchase appropriate equipment for staff May have redundancy implications Communication is becoming impersonal Problems of data security Risk of disclosure of confidential information

Competition

Porter's five forces analysis helps to determine the profit potential of the industry as a whole.

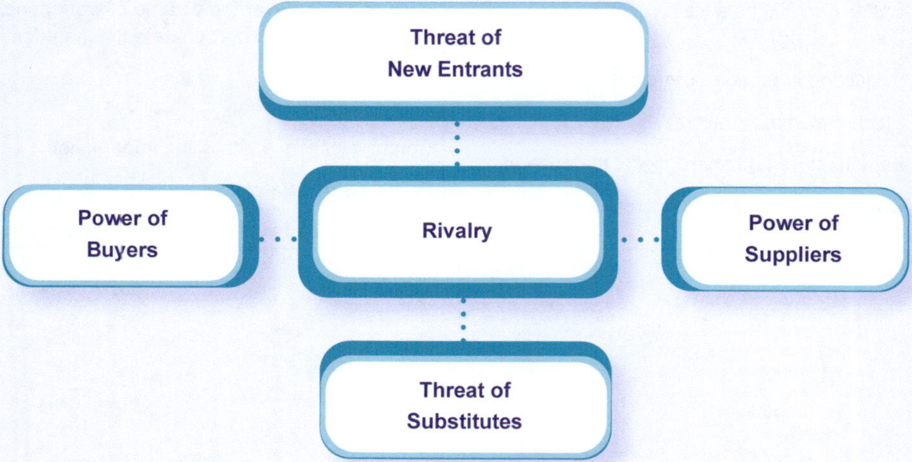

Note: do not confuse rivalry with threat of substitutes.

Threat of new entrants – barriers to entry such as capital requirement, access to distribution channels.

Power of suppliers – dominant supplier controlling prices, switching costs.

Threat of substitutes – another product can be used to satisfy customer needs.

Power of buyers – customer profitability, volume of purchases.

Rivalry – brings pressure to cut costs and improve quality.

The value chain analysis allows us to determine whether (and how) a firm's activities contribute to its competitive advantage.

Porter's Generic Strategies

Cost leadership

This involves the business making a product of similar quality to its rivals, but at a lower cost. This is normally achieved through internal efficiencies.

Differentiation

This strategy involves persuading customers that our product is superior to that of our rivals. It can be done by adding additional features to the product or by altering customer perception of the product through branding and will usually allow the business to charge a premium price.

Focus

This involves aiming at a segment of the market, rather than the market as a whole. A particular group of consumers is identified with the same needs and the business will provide products or services that are tailored to their needs.

Conclusion

Porter argued that businesses needed to adopt one of the above three approaches or they would be 'stuck in the middle', which would make it difficult for them to compete successfully.

Porter's Value Chain

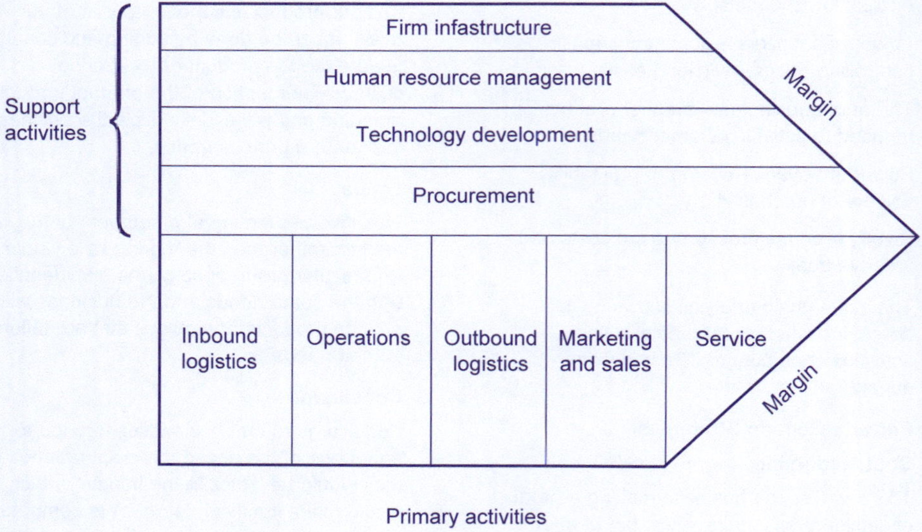

Activity	Description
Inbound logistics	Receiving, handling, storing and distributing inputs to the production system including warehousing, transport, inventory controls.
Operations	Convert resource inputs into final product. Resource inputs are not only materials, but also people especially in the service industry.
Outbound logistics	Storing the product and distributing it to customers including packaging, testing, delivery.
Marketing and sales	Informing customers about the product, persuading them to buy it. Also includes sales administration, sales channels selection and pricing.
Service	Installing products, giving user training, maintaining and repairing them, providing spare parts and breakdown assistance- ensuring the customer enjoys the purchase.
Procurement	How the resources are purchased such as acquiring materials or components.
Technology development	Includes research and development, process automation, product design and resource utilisation.
Human resources	How people within the firm are managed: recruitment, training and incentive schemes.
Firm infrastructure	How the firm is organised: planning, finance and quality control.

SWOT analysis

Once a business has undertaken all of the above analysis, it will understand the key issues in its internal and external environment. All of these issues can be summarised in a SWOT analysis.

S

- The things we are doing well
- The things we are doing well that the competition are not
- Major successes

W

- The things we are doing badly (need to correct or improve
- The things we are not doing but should be
- Major failures

O

- Events or changes in the external environment that can be exploited
- Things likely to go well in the future

T

- Events or changes in the external environment we need to protect ourselves from or defend ourselves against
- Things likely to go badly in the future

Exam focus

- You need to be able to distinguish between political and legal factors.
- Be familiar with the key terms and concepts of economics.
- Look out for recent social and technological trends.
- Be aware of how competitive forces shape the organisation.

chapter

4

Corporate governance, ethics and social responsibility

In this chapter

- Business ethics.
- Code of professional conduct.
- Corporate governance.
- Committees.
- Social responsibility.

Exam focus

- You need to be fluent with definitions of corporate governance and social responsibility.
- As a student-accountant you need to be familiar with ACCA ethical guidelines.
- Be aware of the way companies are run, including functions of the board and various committees.

Business ethics

Definition

Ethics is the analysis of right and wrong and associated responsibility.

Business ethics is the systematic study of moral matters pertaining to business, industry or related activities, institutions or practices and beliefs.

Approaches to ethics.

- A compliance-based approach: organisation acts with regard for and in compliance with the relevant law. Any violations are prevented, detected and punished.
- An integrity-based approach: emphasises managerial responsibility for ethical behaviour, as well as a concern for the law.

Other approaches to ethical dilemmas include:

- **Consequentialist** – a decision is right or wrong depending on the consequences of making that decision. Can broken down into **egoism** and **utilitarianism**.
- **Pluralist** – a decision should cater to the needs of all stakeholders as far as possible, but without seriously compromising the interests of any one group.
- **Relativist** – whether an action is right or wrong depends on the circumstances.
- **Absolutist** – some actions are inherently wrong and can never be justified, regardless of the circumstances. This is linked to deontological ethics – which ignore the consequences of an action.

Source of management's ethical obligations include:

- the law
- government regulations
- ethical codes
- social pressures
- industry and company ethical codes.

Examples of ethical issues are:

- dealing with demands for bribes
- marketing policies (e.g. manufacturing or selling cigarettes and weapons) policies that imply social costs (e.g. pollution of rivers)
- whether or not to export to particular countries.

Ethical codes cover areas including:

- the purpose and values of the organisation
- employees (e.g. its policies on recruitment, redundancy, discrimination)
- customer relations (e.g. relationship of good faith in all agreements)
- shareholders (e.g. protection of investment)
- suppliers (e.g. prompt settlement of bills)
- society or the wider community (e.g. compliance with the spirit of the law as well as the letter).

Benefits of managing ethics in the workplace:

- it has substantially improved society
- cultivates strong teamwork and productivity
- ensures that policies are legal
- promotes a strong public image.

Code of professional conduct

Definition

A profession is a mastery of a specialised skills obtained through a certificated training course that is overseen by a professional association, which means the person has to comply with an ethical code.

ACCA's code of ethics.

- Integrity: being straightforward and honest.
- Objectivity: being fair, unbiased.
- Professional competence and due care: only taking on services one is capable of performing.
- Confidentiality: only disclosing confidential information if there is a legal reason.
- Professional behaviour: avoid bringing the profession into disrepute.

ACCA's roles in promoting ethical behaviour.

- Supporting the accountant in resisting pressure that might distort professional judgment.
- Applying sanctions to those breaching the code.
- Promoting awareness of the code amongst members.

An accountant may face many threats to their ethical principles, including:

- Self interest
- Self review
- Advocacy
- Familiarity
- Intimidation

To deal with these threats, the following safeguards can be used:

ACCA	Businesses
• Ethics training for all professional accountants • Creation of corporate governance requirements • Setting of professional standards • Professional monitoring and disciplinary procedures	• Formal complaints and reporting procedure • Creating ethical culture which includes: **H**onesty **O**penness **T**ransparency **T**rust **E**mpowerment **R**espect

If an accountant uncovers illegal or unethical activities in their organisation, they should:

1 Consult whoever is responsible for ethics in their organisation.

2 Consult their professional body.

3 Consider reporting to the relevant authorities and/or resigning from the engagement.

Corporate governance

Definition

The Cadbury Committee described corporate governance as 'the system by which companies are directed and controlled'.

In a large company it's likely that most shareholders will not play a role in its day-to-day running, which creates the problem of separation of ownership and control.

Reasons of separation	Benefits of separation
Specialist management expertise	Managers can concentrate on the business
Access to more capital	Shareholders earn a return on investment

Perspective on governance.

- Stewardship theory – managers are guardians of the assets and can be dismissed by owners.
- Agency theory – managers must be monitored since they are guided by their own self-interest.
- Stakeholder theory – managers have a duty of care to shareholders and wider community.

Principles of good corporate governance.

- The rights of shareholders: protects and facilitates the exercise of shareholders' rights.
- The equitable treatment of shareholders, including minority and foreign shareholders.
- The role of stakeholders: encourages active co-operation between corporations and stakeholders.
- Disclosure and transparency: timely and accurate disclosure on matters such as financial situation, performance, ownership and governance of the company.
- The responsibility of the board: board's accountability to the company and the shareholders.

Benefits of corporate governance.

- Reduction of risk.
- Better leadership.
- Enhanced performance.
- Improved access to capital markets.
- More shareholder support.

Board of directors

At least half the board should comprise independent non-executive directors (NEDs), who do not engage in day-to-day execution of management decisions.

Role of NEDs.

- Contributing to strategy formulation.
- Monitoring performance by reporting and assessing goal achievement.
- Ensuring robust financial controls and accurate reporting.
- Determining executives remuneration.

Committees

Definition

A committee is a group of people officially delegated to perform a function and who are given appropriate authority.

Purposes of the committee.

- Gathers information.
- Disseminates instructions.
- Generates ideas.
- Combines skills and expertise.
- Gives advice and recommendations.
- Coordinates efforts.

Types of committees.

- Ad-hoc – solving short-term problems.
- Standing – permanent, formed to aid in problem-solving.
- Sub-committee – relieves a permanent committee of routine work.
- Joint – coordinates activities of two or more committees.
- Executive – has power to govern and administer.
- Steering – oversees a major project.
- Work safety – looks after working methods and conditions.
- Ethics – oversees working practices and procedures.
- Audit – comprised of NEDs, reviews financial controls and integrity of financial statements.
- Remuneration – comprised of at least three NEDs, sets out remuneration for executive directors.
- Nomination – ensures composition of the board is balanced.

Role of committee chair.

- Keeping the meeting to a schedule and agenda.
- Maintaining order.
- Ensuring correct procedures are followed.
- Ensuring all parties have a reasonable opportunity to express their view.
- Checking and signing off the minutes.

Role of committee secretary.

- Making administrative arrangements prior to the meeting.
- Preparing and issuing meeting agenda.
- Assisting the chairperson.
- Making notes and preparing minutes.
- Dealing with correspondence.

Social responsibility

Definition

Social responsibility is a duty to all stakeholders of the undertaking to make decisions in a way that takes into account the interests of the environment and society as a whole.

Benefits of social responsibility.

- Attracting customers by meeting social expectation.
- Reducing operational risk.
- Identifying new market opportunities.
- Retaining employees.
- Reducing legal costs.

chapter

5

Accounting function and financial procedures

In this chapter

- Regulations covering accounting function.
- Accounting profession.
- Financial procedures.
- Coordination between accounting and other business functions.

Exam focus

- Make sure you understand the content of financial statements.
- You need to have an overview of main regulatory bodies and their requirement.
- Financial procedures are a key topic in the exam.

Definition

Accounting is a way of recording, reporting and analysing the financial transactions of the business. Accountants provide information for decision-making purposes.

Regulations covering accounting function

Responsibility to regulatory authorities.

- Companies House (e.g. submission of financial statement for inspection by interested parties).
- Tax authorities (e.g. HMRC for VAT, PAYE, corporation tax).
- Financial services (e.g. stock exchange for listed companies).
- Regulators, where appropriate (e.g. Charities Commission, Ofcom).

Therefore accounting records must contain:

- details of all money received and spent
- a record of assets and liabilities
- statement of stocks at the end of year
- statements of all goods sold and purchased.

Financial statements include:

- statement of financial position (balance sheet)
- statement of profit or loss (income statement)
- statement of cash flows
- statement of recognised gains and losses.
- integrated and sustainability reports.

Users of financial statements.

- Managers.
- Shareholders.
- Audit firms.
- General public.
- Governmental authorities.

Companies Act 2006 sets out that financial statements have to give a "true and fair view".

- Properly prepared in accordance with accounting standards.
- Not misleading, information is of sufficient quantity and quality.
- Following generally accepted accounting practice.

Consequences of compliance failure.

- It's a criminal offence and may lead to prosecution of directors.
- Company may be fined by tax authorities.
- Qualified auditing report damages reputation and makes it hard to borrow money.
- Poor relationships with customers and suppliers due to inadequate recordkeeping.

Bodies governing the accounting function

IFRS Foundation supervises the development of international standards and guidance. It's a parent entity of:

- International Accounting Standards Board (IASB): aims to develop a single set of quality, understandable and enforceable accounting standards.
- IFRS Interpretation Committee (IFRS IC): reviews widespread accounting issues and provides guidance.
- IFRS Advisory Council (IFRS AC): consults the users of financial information and offers advice to the IFRS Foundation.

Accounting profession

Structure of accounting function:

- Financial accounting
  - Maintaining books of prime entry
  - Preparatory work for financial statements
  - Providing financial report to management
- Management accounting
  - Setting budgets and budgetary control
  - Analysing company's performance
  - Investment appraisal
- Treasury
  - Cash management
  - Monitoring investment and borrowing
  - Foreign currency trading
  - Managing tax affairs
- Auditing
  - Evaluating the strength of internal controls
  - Recommending operational improvement
  - Reviewing financial reports

Financial procedures

Purchasing cycle

Requisition	Deciding what goods need to be ordered Authorised person to place the request with purchasing department
Ordering	Obtaining quotations from suppliers Negotiating beneficial payment terms
Goods received	Inspection of quality and quantity of goods
Invoice received	Checking the invoice for correctness
Invoice recorded	Making appropriate accounting records
Payment made	Usually by BACS

Sales cycle

Order received	Could be by phone or e-mail Need to confirm that person has authority to order on customers behalf
Order processed	Verifying customer credit status Checking whether goods are in stock
Goods dispatched	Obtain confirmation of goods delivery
Invoicing	Providing detailed breakdown of items and prices
Recording	Making sure records are correct and complete
Payment received	Credit control will oversee timely receipts

Wages cycle

Hours worked	Received on paper timesheets or through electronic systems
Overtime	Needs to be authorised by the manager
Pay rate	Could be hourly or daily, to be confirmed with HR
Calculation	Gross pay may also include expenses and benefits-in-kind
Deductions	Statutory ones (tax, NI), student loans, previous overpayments
Net pay	To be transferred to employee's bank account or given in cash

Cash system

Receipt	Cash has to be paid in to the bank within an appropriate time BACS transfers to be allocated to customer account
Payment	To suppliers by BACS, CHAPS or cheque To staff (salaries) To governmental authorities in respect of tax liabilities
Petty cash	Necessary for small purchases (e.g. stamps) Every issue has to be accompanied by a receipt Should be reconciled on a regular basis

Inventory system

This is a combination of purchasing and sales cycles, with the addition of warehousing responsibilities.

Goods in store include:

- raw materials
- work in progress
- finished goods.

Coordination between accounting and other business functions

To achieve effective performance, the organisation must align the activities of its various functions. Accounting, being a central function, plays a vital part in coordinating efforts.

Department	Areas of interaction
Purchasing	Establishing credit terms Monitoring payments Inventory and cost control
Production	Cost measurement and overhead allocation Budgeting (e.g. units, quantity) Achieving efficiency and economy
HR	Recruitment and training expenditure Salary payment, estimating PAYE liabilities Reward plans, tax-efficient benefit packages
IT	Systems design and development Improving access to information Incorporating new technology into operations
Customer services	Pricing additional services (e.g. maintenance) Assessing costs of product failures Qualitative feedback on operations
Marketing	Advertising budgets Product pricing Estimating market share

chapter

6

Auditing and fraud prevention

In this chapter

- Internal and external audit.
- Internal controls.
- Dealing with fraud.
- IT systems security.

Exam focus

- Be prepared to identify the differences between external and internal audit.
- You might be required to choose which control measures are most appropriate in a certain situation.
- Be aware of different types of fraudulent activities and possible remedies against them.

Internal and external audit

Definition

Internal auditing is an independent activity, established by management, to examine and evaluate organisational risk management processes and control systems and make recommendations for improvement.

External auditing is an independent examination of the financial statement to see whether it gives true and fair view of company's affairs.

Internal audit

Purpose	Scope	Limitations
Part of good corporate governance initiatives. Enables performance improvement through risk assessment. Helps to set corporate objectives. Aids in design and monitoring of performance measures.	Reviewing internal controls and financial reports. Reviewing risk management systems. Carrying out special assignments (e.g. fraud investigations). Conducting operational reviews (e.g. efficiency improvements). Review of compliance with legislation and internal policies.	Independence problem: though employed by management, have to give an objective opinion on how the company is managed. Will only succeed if properly staffed and resourced. If fraud is identified, they may be unwilling to disclose it for fear of the repercussions (e.g. loss of jobs, company collapse).

Internal auditors are accountable to the Board of Directors or, in better cases, to the Audit committee that will act as an interface between directors and management to reduce the problem of independence.

External audit

An unqualified opinion (i.e. statements give true and fair view) makes them more reliable. Existence of external auditors may also encourage employees to document their work properly and dissuade them from fraud, as they know they will be checked.

Advantages	Disadvantages
Disputes between management are more easily settled (e.g. accounting treatments concerning provisions). Unqualified audit report facilitates change of ownership. Easier to obtain finance as past trading records have been confirmed. Managers can benefit from auditors advice on improving business efficiency.	The audit fee could be a burden. Causes disruption to the operations of the accounts department.

In the process of their work external auditors perform two types of tests.

- Test of controls identify the extent to which internal controls could be relied upon.
- Substantive testing is aimed to substantiating the figures and balances.

Differences between internal and external audit

	Internal audit	External audit
Roles	To advise management the strength of internal controls and to protect the organisation against loss.	To provide an opinion to the shareholders on whether the financial statements give a true and fair view.
Legal basis	Not a legal requirement, but is highly recommended by UK Corporate Governance Code for listed companies.	Legal requirement for medium-size and large companies, and public bodies.
Scope of work	Determined by management, covers all areas of operations.	Determined by the auditor, focuses on finance.
Approach	Evaluates systems of controls, tests operations of system, makes recommendations for improvement.	Tests underlying transactions that form the basis of the financial statements.
Employed by	Company directors, with reduces their independence.	Firm of accountants, fully independent, appointed by shareholders.

Internal controls

Definition

Internal control is a process designed and initiated by management to provide reasonable assurance about the achievement of the entity's objectives with regards to reliability of financial reporting, effectiveness and efficiency of operations and compliance with laws and regulations.

Internal checks are checks on day-to-day transactions. They prevent 'bad things' from happening, e.g. fraud.

It is a responsibility of management to establish proper control arrangements. The UK Corporate Governance Code recommends that controls should be reviewed at least annually with subsequent report to shareholders.

Components of internal controls.

- **Control environment**: overall attitude of managers to internal controls.
- **The entity's risk assessment process**: how the company identifies and responds to risks.
- **Information systems and communication**: procedures to process transactions and maintain control over assets, liabilities and balances.
- **Control activities**: policies to ensure management directives are carried out.
- **The entity's process to monitor the system of internal control**: assessment of internal control performance over time.

Examples of specific control activities include those relating to:

- **Authorisation** to confirm the validity of a transaction.
- **Reconciliations** to address the completeness or accuracy of transactions.
- **Verifications** to address the completeness, accuracy or validity of transactions.

- **Physical or logical controls** to prevent theft of assets or data.
- **Segregation of duties** to reduce opportunity for any person to commit and conceal fraud in the normal course of their duties.

Types of control:

- Preventive (e.g. segregation of duties, screening of new personnel).
- Detective (e.g. reconciliation, supervision, stock takes).
- Corrective (e.g. data back-ups, follow-up procedures).

Aims of internal checks:

- Segregate duties so omissions could be traced.
- Create and preserve records.
- Review procedures to identify bottlenecks in the flow of information.
- Prevent and detect the possibility of fraud and error.

Dealing with fraud

Definition

Fraud is an intentional act involving the usage of deception to obtain an unjust or illegal advantage. It's a criminal offence punishable by imprisonment.

Prerequisites of fraud:

- dishonesty – individual's pre-disposition to act in ways which contravenes accepted ethical social, organisational and legal norms for fair and honest dealing. Arises from personal factors (e.g. need for achievement, status) or cultural factors (e.g. bribes are acceptable in some countries)
- motivation – involves a calculation whether a given action is worthwhile. Individual weighs up the potential rewards the potential sanctions
- opportunity – this refers to a "loophole" in the law or control systems that allows

fraudulent activity to go undetected or makes the risk of detection acceptably low.

Fraud could be committed by:

- management (e.g. window dressing, misappropriation of assets)
- employees (e.g. teeming and lading, payroll fraud, skimming schemes)
- third parties (e.g. false billing, advance fee fraud, pyramid schemes).

Implications of fraud:

- company collapse
- adverse publicity
- reduced profits as company has fewer assets
- financial statements do not give true and fair view, leads to a qualified audit report
- distorted performance results make it hard for managers to make business decisions.

The responsibility for preventing fraud can be split between:

- duties of the board of directors: UK Corporate Governance Code requires directors to maintain a sound system of internal control
- duties of employees: specific duties are set out in their contract of employment, but there also is an implied duty to act honestly and to report suspected actual frauds
- role of external auditors: they carry insurance against being sued for negligence. If in the course of audit they decide that the matter is significant enough, they can report it to an appropriate authority in the public interest. If the financial statements are affected by fraud, they should qualify the report accordingly.

Money laundering

Money laundering is the exchange of 'dirty' money and assets that have been criminally obtained for 'clean' money and assets that have no clear link to criminal activity.

Money laundering follows three distinct phases:

- Placement
- Layering
- Integration

Typical money laundering regulations recognise three main offences:

- Laundering: acquiring, using, investing or handling criminally obtained property.
- Failure to report proof or suspicion of money laundering.
- Tipping off suspected money launderers.

The controls and procedures required by law will often include, amongst others:

- Identification of large or unusual transactions.
- Scrutinising of unusual patterns of transactions.
- Taking steps to ensure all customers can be identified.
- Creation of the role of Money Laundering Reporting Officer.

It is also important that a business has a defined reporting process for any suspected money laundering. This will normally involve:

- employees reporting suspicious activity to the Money Laundering Reporting Officer
- the Money Laundering Reporting Officer investigating further
- if there are grounds for reasonable suspicion, Money Laundering Reporting Officer reporting to the relevant authorities.

IT systems security

The use of computerised accounting packaging has become the norm.

Features of the automated system:

- uniform processing of transactions (e.g. automatic allocation of Dr and Cr)
- allow to gain an overview of the business as it integrates all operations
- increased supervision as there is an audit trail
- can analyse the data in accordance with user requirements.

Risks to data.

- Human errors are inevitable.
- Technical malfunctions (e.g. systems crash results in lost or corrupted data).
- Natural disasters (e.g. flood, fire).
- Sabotage or espionage (e.g. attempt to damage or steal data for commercial gain).
- Malicious damage (e.g. by hackers, disaffected employees).

Principles of data security.

- Use individual and complex passwords.
- Secure communication channels (e.g. firewalls).
- Back up information on a regular basis.
- Have a contingency plan.
- Do not leave documents in accessible places.
- Do not open suspicious emails (e.g. danger of viruses).

Types of IT control

General IT controls – support the continued proper operation of the IT environment, including effective functioning of the information processing controls and the integrity of information in the information system. General controls include: physical controls, hardware and software configuration, disaster recovery, technical support.

Information processing controls – relate to the processing of information in IT applications or manual processes that directly address risks to the integrity of information.

These controls will vary from system to system, but are often designed to ensure:

- **completeness** – has all necessary data been input?
- **authorisation** – is the person inputting the data authorised to do so?
- **identification** – can the person inputting the information be uniquely identified?
- **validity** – is the information being input by the user valid?
- **forensic checks** – is the information being input by the user mathematically accurate?

chapter

7

Leadership, management and teamwork

In this chapter

- Introduction to management.
- Theories of management.
- Authority, responsibility, power concepts.
- Leadership.
- Individual and group behaviour.
- Teamwork.

Exam focus

- You need to be able to distinguish between leadership and management.
- You need to have a sound understanding of leadership and management theories, their rationale and application to real life situations.
- Learn Belbin and Tuckman's theories as you might need to identify a role based on its description or recognise the stage of team development in a question.

Introduction to management

Definition

Management is the effective use and coordination of resources such as capital, plant and labour to achieve objectives with maximum efficiency.

Supervision is using authority given by the manager for planning and controlling the work of the group.

Functions of management **(Fayol)**

- Plan – setting goals, preparing schedules for achieving targets.
- Organise – allocating tasks and responsibility, delegating duties.
- Command – instruct subordinates as to how to carry out the tasks.
- Coordinate – integrating work flows, goal congruence.
- Control – monitoring and measuring performance, taking corrective actions.

Role of a supervisor

- Interface between management and staff.
- Dealing with shop floor problems and customer complaints.
- Has to possess technical knowledge of the operations.
- Controls work by means of day-to-day, detailed information.
- Filters communication by conveying upwards suggestions and feedback, passing downward policies and instructions.

Theories of management

Classical theories

Taylors's scientific management focused on planning, standardising and improving human effort at the operative level as to maximize the output with minimum input. His principles are:

- science of work – best way to do a job
- scientific selection & development of workers – training each to be first class at what they do
- all work has to be planned, measured and controlled – standardisation
- equal division of work and responsibility between workers and management.

Practical application of the classical approach:

- focusing on efficiency of operations (stopwatch system, standard times for producing an item)
- managers are responsible for planning, workers just follow the instructions
- narrow specialisation (workers performs a single operation)
- emphasis on monetary rewards.

Criticisms:

- assembly line moves at the speed of the slowest operator
- people are treated as costs rather than resources
- fails to engage the creativity of individual workers, is highly impersonal.

Relevance today

- They are still in use in labour intensive manufacturing, fast food chains & call centres.
- It is recognized that in today's knowledge economy staff can make a significant contribution to the business by making suggestions.

- In professional occupation there is seldom "one best way" as flexibility in approach is highly valued.

Modern writers

Drucker – instead of breaking away from the classical school he adjusted it by adding a more "human" side to management.

Management should:

- fulfil the specific purpose and mission of the organization (by setting goals)
- make work productive (by using teamwork) and the work achieving (rewards to be tailored to individual needs)
- manage social impacts and social responsibility (long-term view of organisational impact).

Drucker argued that all managers perform five basic operations, the main focus being economic performance through setting objectives and controlling performance.

- set objectives – determine what should be done and communicate it to staff
- organise – divide work into manageable units
- motivate and communicate – establish a team
- establish yardsticks – focus on performance measurement and appraisal
- develop people – keeping people' skills up-to-date.

Mintzberg challenged the classical view of management by saying that systematic planning is not always possible in a rapidly changing environment. Majority of manager's work has to do with judgement and intuition which can only be obtained from experience.

Category	Role	Explanation
Interpersonal	Figurehead	Symbolic role, performing ceremonial duties
	Leader	Fostering commitment by inspiring and motivating staff
	Liaison	Networking, developing contacts
Informational	Monitor	Collecting information from internal & external environment
	Disseminator	Spreading the information to subordinates
	Spokesperson	PR capacity, informs the public of company's intentions
Decision-making	Entrepreneur	Looking for new opportunities, initiating projects
	Disturbance handler	Dealing with problems and unexpected pressures
	Resource allocator	Deciding on the best way to allocate funds, people etc.
	Negotiator	Participating in bargaining process

Authority, responsibility, power concepts

Definition

Authority is a legitimate right to give orders.

Responsibility is an obligation placed on a person to fulfil a task.

Power is an ability to exert influence.

Accountability is the need to justify your actions.

Delegation is a process of transferring the authority to a subordinate.

Types of authority:

Line – down the vertical chain, manager over subordinate.

Staff – based on giving specialist advice to the same level employee.

Functional – setting procedures outside the departmental lines.

Sources of authority

- Rational-legal – efficient, based on rules and procedures.
- Traditional – status-centred, based on custom & practice.
- Charismatic – due to special qualities of personality.

Authority and Responsibility should always correspond.

- Authority/no responsibility – creates tyrant.
- Responsibility/ no authority – leads to irresponsible behaviour.

Sources of power

- Legitimate.
- Reward.
- Coercive.
- Referent.
- Expert.
- Resource.

Leadership

Definition

Leadership – interpersonal influence directed towards the achievement of goals.

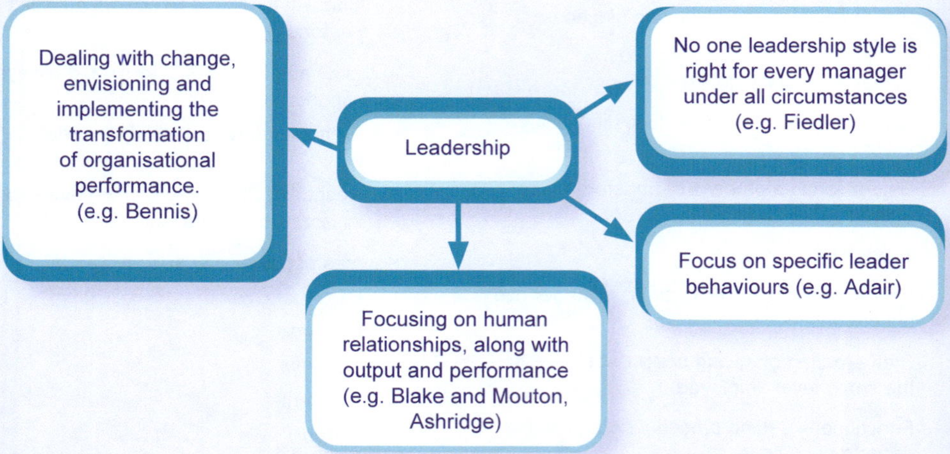

Leadership and Management

- The manager administers; the leader innovates.
- The manager relies on control; the leader inspires trust.
- The manager has his eye on the bottom line; the leader has his eye on the horizon.

Trait theory – leaders are born and not made

- Physical traits – drive, energy, appearance.
- Personality traits – adaptability, enthusiasm, self-confidence.
- Social traits – cooperation, tact, and courtesy.

Action-centred leadership (Adair) – focused on what leader does.

Fiedler's theory – leadership style depends on the situation.

Psychologically distant manager

- ✓ Formal staff contact
- ✓ Emphasises efficient task completion
- ✓ Reserved

Psychologically close manager

- ✓ Informal links with staff
- ✓ Focused on good human relationships
- ✓ Open and approachable

Favourable situation

- The **leader** is liked and trusted by the group
- The **tasks** in the group are clearly defined
- The **power** of the leader to reward and punish with organisational backing is high

Psychologically distant style works best when situation is very favourable or very unfavourable.

Psychologically close style works best when the situation is moderately favourable.

Bennis

Manager – does the things right.

Leader – does the right things.

Transactional leader	Transformational leader
• Gives reward in exchange for compliance • Builds on man's need to make a living • Is preoccupied with power and position • Focuses on tactical issues • Strives to work effectively within current systems • Supports actions that guarantee short-term profits	• Creates new directions • Builds on a man's need for meaning • Is orientated toward long-term goals • Focuses more on missions and strategies • Releases human potential – identifying and developing new talent • Redesigns jobs to make them meaningful and challenging

Leadership abilities

- Management of attention: give focus, create a vision.
- Management of meaning: effective communication.
- Management of trust: being consistent and honest.
- Management of self: emotional wisdom.

Blake and Mouton

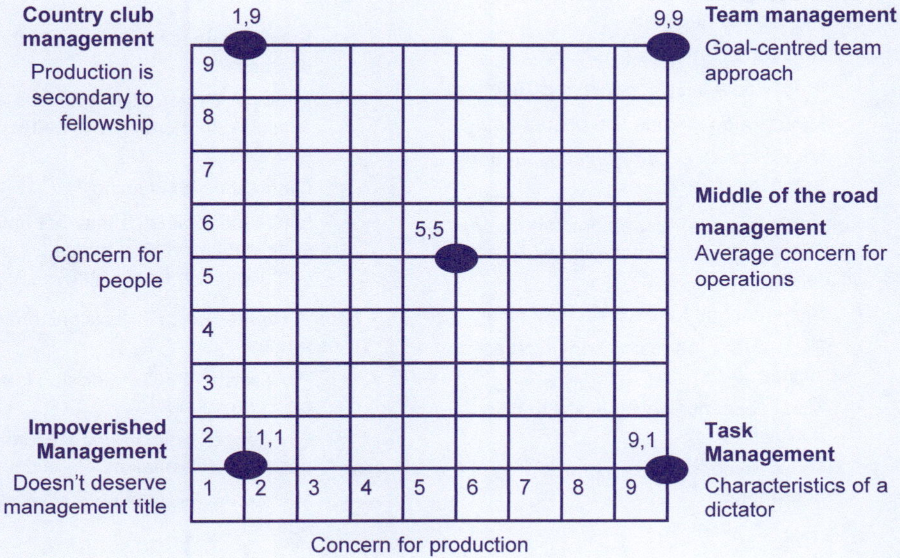

Ashridge distinguished between four styles of leadership.

Tells (autocratic) – instruction are to be obeyed without question.

- Appropriate in crisis situations.
- Plus: works best when work is repetitive.
- Minus: subordinates feel unimportant.
- Minus: resulting compliance is far from true commitment.

Sells (persuasive) – decisions are made by the managers, but subordinates need to accept them.

- Plus: reasons for decisions are clear.
- Plus: loyalty to the company increases slightly.
- Minus: communication is still mainly downwards.
- Minus: acceptance does not signify agreement.

Consults (participates) – manager retains the power of final say, but makes the decision after the discussion with the whole team.

- Plus: people feel more part of the process.
- Plus: more alternative solutions are available so the choice is better informed.
- Minus: time-consuming.
- Minus: subordinates may not have sufficient knowledge to make a valuable contribution to discussion.

Joins (democratic) – decisions are made by consensus.

- Plus: "ownership" of decision leads to high commitment.
- Plus: expert opinion and customer perspective are taken into account.
- Minus: may undermine manager's authority.

- Minus: conflict is inevitable making consensus hard to reach.

Individual and group behaviour

Factors that influence behaviour:

- Motivation – why people choose to do one thing rather than another.
- Perception – stimuli from the environment are organised into meaningful patterns.
- Attitudes – persistent feelings and behavioural tendencies.
- Personality – characteristic ways of thinking and behaving that distinguish individuals.
- Roles – patterns of behaviour that people tend to adopt when faced with certain situations.

Behaviour types

- Passive – believe that rights of another person are more important than yours (e.g. "Would you kindly do this urgent task, if you don't mind").
- Aggressive – violates other person's right (e.g. "You must do it immediately otherwise…").
- Assertive – respecting right of both parties (e.g. "Would you be able to do it now?").

Role theory

- Role ambiguity – individuals are unsure what role they are to play, or others are.
- Role conflict – there is a clash between differing roles.
- Role incompatibility – individual's expectations about their role are different from group expectations.
- Role signs – visible indications of the role.
- Role set – people who support a lead person in a major role.
- Role behaviour – some types of behaviour are expected in certain roles.

Definition

Group is any collection of people who perceive themselves to be a group.

Factors that make a cohesive group.

- Leadership.
- Right mix of skills.
- Clear objectives and commitment to shared goals.
- Team identity.
- Team solidarity.

Advantage of cohesive groups.

- Teamwork, participation.
- Creativity, better problem-solving.
- Better communication.
- Support and good social atmosphere.
- Conflicts are easily resolved.

Teamwork

Definition

A team is a formal group, that has a leader, a distinctive culture and is geared towards a final result.

The purpose of the team is to solve complex problems.

Teams contribute to organisational success due to:

- synergy (2+2=5) combined efforts of individuals are greater than the sum of individual efforts
- cooperation creates better results in terms of efficiency and quality
- combination of different field of expertise, having complimentary skills
- good coordination of activities.

Team	**Group**
Share a common goal	Interests change frequently
High level of commitment	Membership is often temporary
Team spirit	People negotiate and accommodate
Healthy competition	Politics is common

Types of teams.

Multi-skilled teams: bring together individuals who can perform any of the group's tasks.

Multi-disciplinary teams: individuals with different specialisation exchange their skills and experience.

Belbin's team roles

1 Leader – co-ordinating (not imposing) and operating through others – balanced, disciplined.

2 Shaper – committed to the task, may be aggressive and challenging, will also always promote activity – dominant, extrovert.

3 Plant – thoughtful and thought-provoking – introvert, creatively intelligent.

4 Monitor-evaluator – analytically criticizes others' ideas, brings group down to earth – analytically intelligent.

5 Resource-investigator – not a new ideas person, but tends to pick up others' ideas and adds to them; is usually a social type of person who often acts as a bridge to the outside world – extrovert networker.

6 Company worker – turns general ideas into specifics; practical and efficient, tends to be an administrator handling the scheduling aspects – essential organiser.

7 Team worker –- concerned with the relationships within the group, is supportive and tends to defuse potential conflict situations – diplomatic.

8 Finisher – unpopular, but a necessary individual; the progress chaser who ensures that timetables are met.

9 Expert – possesses specialised knowledge and skills that are in rare supply within the team, dedicated, self-starting.

Stages of team development (Tuckman)

1 Forming – group is just a collection of individuals who define the purpose of group. There is a lot of uncertainty and doubt among members, however they feel enthusiastic and are excited about the forthcoming challenge.

2 Storming – conflict stage, preconceptions are challenged, attitudes and behaviour are confronted and rejected. There is a lot of hostility towards the task within the group, members compete for their chosen roles.

3 Norming – group settles down into a routine, establishes the process for making decisions, agrees on acceptable behavioural patterns, members learn to trust each other.

4 Performing – people are operating to their full potential, everyone is focused on the task. The group itself is strong, loyal and cohesive.

5 Dorming – if the group gets too cosy, there is a danger that it will become complacent, lose interest in results and will exist only for self preservation. Groupthink effect occurs at this stage.

6 Adjourning (mourning) – the group has completed its work and will disband.

Symptoms of groupthink	Ways to combat Groupthink
Discussion is limited to only few alternatives Initially proposed solutions are not re-examined at a later point Group is overly confident, no need for contingency plan	Changing group composition (adding a new member or taking someone out) Expanding the scope of the task, setting tougher targets Providing extra challenges

Effective teams

Evaluating team effectiveness.

- Effectiveness.
- Efficiency.
- Team-members satisfaction.
- Creativity.

Blockages to an effective team (Woodcock).

- Inappropriate leadership.
- Unqualified membership.
- Unconstructive climate.
- Poor achievement.
- Low creative capacity.

Ineffective teams

- These can damage the company when:
- Team goals differ from those of the organisation.
- Teams become too inward looking.
- There is pressure to conform to group norms.
- There is be a lack of individual responsibility.
- There is too much social interaction.
- There is a lack of individual performance measurement.

Five key aspects of successful teams (Peters and Waterman).

- Small numbers.
- Limited duration – task specific.
- Voluntary membership.
- Informal communication, no status barriers.
- Action-oriented.

Rewarding the team:

Methods	Problems
Based on individual contribution	Results rely on collaboration rather than individual effort so the input of each employee is difficult to isolate
Equally	Some people may slack-off whereas others "live to work"
Based on prior agreement	Its is hard to predict the complexity of tasks in advance, often in practice a person would need to contribute more than initially anticipated

chapter

8

Motivation

In this chapter

- Overview of motivation.
- Theories of motivation.
- Incentive schemes.

Overview of motivation

Definition

Motivation is the internal psychological process of initiating, energizing, directing and maintaining goal-directed behaviour (Buchanan & Huczynski, 1997).

Motivation is the urge to achieve goals, the drive to excel. It is concerned with why people choose to do one thing rather than another and with the amount of effort or intensity of action that people put into their activities.

Satisfaction on the other hand is about being content. Low morale is often associated with dissatisfaction.

Benefits of motivation

Organisational perspective	Individual perspective
• Employees work harder and make fewer mistakes • They want more feedback and are prepared to change and improve • Make more suggestions and are ready to use their creative potential	• People feel happier in their job, work becomes enjoyable • They are less stressed, they feel pride in their abilities and achievement • Career prospects and employability improve

Theories of motivation

Maslow's hierarchy of needs

Maslow's heirarchy of needs

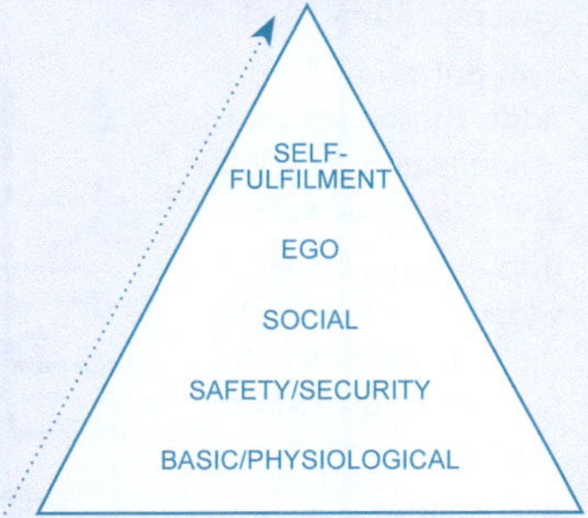

Criticisms of Maslow.

- Needs could have a different priority or be of equal value.
- Hierarchy is focused on the individual and ignores the impact of the group interaction.
- Cultural differences are not taken into account.
- Some jobs don't have a potential to meet all of the above needs.

Herzberg two-factor theory

The hygiene factors are those which deal with non-job related features, they are purely preventative and can pre-empt dissatisfaction. Motivators are mostly non-financial and will encourage people to work harder and take on extra responsibility.

Hygiene factors are merely a platform, in themselves they do not motivate, but if undermined they preclude staff from being satisfied in their job.

Herzberg's theory of job design

He suggested that repetitive, menial jobs are outdated and by redesigning them management can increase the job satisfaction of their staff.

- **Job enrichment:** adds challenges and responsibility to a job, staff are empowered.

- **Job enlargement:** widens the range of the job and enables movement away from specialisation.

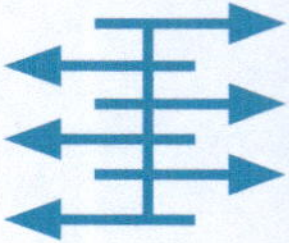

- **Job rotation:** a number of tasks is completed by a team of workers, gives variety.

McGregor's Theory X and Y

The managerial assumptions about their staff can be subdivided into two categories.

Theory X	Theory Y
• Human beings have an inherent dislike of work and will avoid it if possible. • People must be coerced, controlled, directed, or threatened with punishment to get them to put effort in to achieve organisational objectives.	• Physical and mental effort in work is natural, people not only accept but seek responsibility. • Staff will exercise self-direction and self-control to achieve objectives to which they are committed.
• People prefer to be directed, wish to avoid responsibility, have relatively little ambition, and want security above all else.	• People possess a high level of imagination, ingenuity, and creativity. They can therefore help to solve organisational problems.

Incentive schemes

Well designed reward system should:

- attract and retain staff
- increase willingness to accept change
- encourage desirable behaviour
- reflect the nature of the job
- control salary costs.

Types of incentive schemes.

- Performance related pay (e.g. piece rate, commission).
- Bonus schemes.
- Profit sharing.

Financial motivators.

- Maslow – pay can be used to satisfy a range of needs either directly (for lower level needs) or indirectly (for higher level needs).
- Herzberg – pay is normally a hygiene factor but could also be viewed as a motivator where it gives recognition for work well done.
- Vroom – pay is one of the rewards that may be valued by an individual.
- McGregor – Theory X people are purely financially motivated, Theory Y people seek much more than money from their jobs.

Non-financial motivators

- Feedback – increases confidence and allows development of skill.
- Participation – empowering staff, sharing decision-making responsibility.
- Autonomy – opportunity to exercise discretion and self-management.

chapter

9

Learning, training and development

In this chapter

- Learning.
- Training and development.
- Learning organisation.

Exam focus

- You need to be familiar with main theories of learning.
- Be aware how different training methods could be used.
- Appreciate the relevance of the learning organisation approach.

Learning

Definition

Learning is the process of acquiring knowledge, which leads to a change of behaviour.

Experiential learning (Kolb) theory suggests that learning is a continuous cycle with four stages all of which have to be completed for the new knowledge to be fully acquired.

Kolb's experiential learning theory:

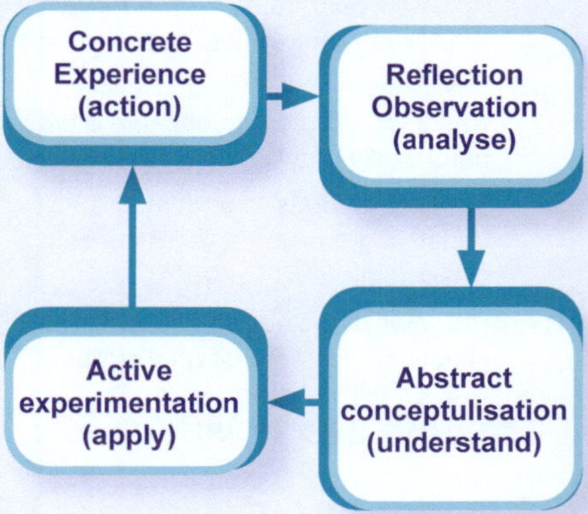

Honey and Mumford learning styles.

- Activist – open to new experiences, "hands-on", enjoys teamwork and role-plays.
- Reflector – prefers to observe others before taking action, likes homework.
- Theorist – needs to understand underlying principles, learns best in a classroom.
- Pragmatists – keen to deal with real situations, learns best on the job.

Training and development

Definition

Training – planned and systematic modification of behaviour through learning events which enables individuals to achieve a high level of knowledge, skills and competence.

Development – growth of person's ability and potential through learning and educational experiences.

Education – process of developing knowledge, skills and character required in all aspects of life.

Stages of the training process

Identifying training needs	Compare standards in the job description to individual capabilities Look at performance results compared to organisational goals Analyse employee requests Results of manager' observation Collect customer feedback Caused by change (e.g. new IT system) Specify knowledge, skills and competences to be acquired
Sets objectives for training	These should be: • Specific – well-defined • Measurable – expressed in numerical terms • Attainable – within person's capability • Relevant – aligned with overall organisational objectives • Timely – should contain a deadline

Programme, design and delivery	Consideration of different training methods: • On the job (e.g. coaching, mentoring, work shadowing, apprenticeship) • Home study, computer-interactive learning • Qualifications and courses • Devote sufficient resources to the process • Equipment (e.g. books, computer access) • Money (e.g. cost of the course, reallocating workload) • Time (e.g. duration of training) Delivery methods include: • In-house (e.g. by Training department) • External (e.g. by specialist provider) Monitor attendance Provide access to practical training-related situations
Validation of the training programme	Hamblin's five levels: • Reaction of the trainee (e.g. how enjoyable it was) • Knowledge acquired (e.g. tests) • Transfer on the job (e.g. dealing with practical tasks) • Organisational efficiency (e.g. productivity improvement) • Ultimate value (e.g. long-term benefits)

Learning organisation

Definition

A learning organisation is an organisation where individuals continually expand their capacity to create results they truly desire, where new thinking patterns are nurtured, and where people are continuously learning.

Features of a learning organisation.

- Generate and transfer knowledge throughout the organisation.
- Learn from others and from past experience.
- Tolerate risk and failure as learning opportunities.
- Have a systematic, ongoing, collective and scientific approach to problem-solving.

Role of manager in a learning organisation.

- All members should be involved in strategy formulation.
- Information is seen as a resource, not a power tool.
- Creating a central knowledge database.
- Developing "internal customer" ideology.
- Structuring the organisation as to promote flexibility.
- Providing opportunities for learning.

chapter

10

Appraisal

In this chapter

- Purpose of appraisal.
- Barriers to effective appraisal.

Exam focus

- You need to have a sound understanding of the purpose and the process of appraisal.
- Be able to recognise what makes an appraisal system ineffective.

Purpose of appraisal

Definition

Appraisal is a regular and systematic review of performance and assessment of potential with an aim of producing an action programme to develop both work and individual.

Purpose of appraisal is to review:

- performance: compare results achieved against standards set
- potential: identifying talented staff
- pay: discussing remuneration package.

Criteria for assessment:

- volume and quality of work
- competence and knowledge of operations
- management skills
- personal qualities and work attitude
- commitment and motivation.

Objectives of appraisal

From organisational point of view	From individual's point of view
Establishing the results staff have to deliver	Determines future promotional opportunities
Identifies training and development needs	Gives recognition for work well done
Encourages communication	Serves as a basis for increase in remuneration
Aids personnel planning	Formal opportunity to ask for guidance
Creates supportive organisational culture	Chance to contribute to goal-setting process

Conducting appraisal

Preparation.

- Manager needs to be familiar with company policy (e.g. frequency of appraisal).
- Collect relevant documentation (e.g. appraisal form).
- Collect feedback about employee performance (e.g. 360° review).
- Ask the staff to fill in the self-appraisal form.
- Prepare the agenda for discussion.
- Arrange suitable environment (e.g. confidentiality, timing).

Appraisal interview.

- Importance of interviewing skills (e.g. questioning, listening, paying attention).
- Employing appropriate communication strategy (tell and sell, tell and listen, problem-solving).
- Both parties have to have a chance to ask questions.
- Agree objectives for the next period.
- Both parties sign the review form.

Follow-up.

- Giving training and support if requested.
- Filing paperwork with HR.

Barriers to effective appraisal

Common problems encountered with appraisals include:

- appraisal as a confrontation: parties are sidetracked by differences and disagreement
- appraisal as a judgement: managers just delivers his/her verdict, no chance of appeal
- appraisal as a chat: not taken seriously, seen as a waste of time

- appraisal as bureaucracy: impersonal form-filling exercise
- appraisal as an annual event: just a ceremony, has no purpose
- appraisal as unfinished business: only looks at recent events and ignores all else.

Features of effective appraisal system:

- relevance: needs to be useful for the individual and the organisation
- fairness: objective assessment criteria
- serious intent: full managerial commitment
- cooperation: is a participative, problem-solving process
- efficiency: easy to administer, not time-consuming.

Evaluating effectiveness of appraisal:

- cost/benefit analysis
- asking staff and managers for their opinion
- investigating whether improvement resulted from it
- checking promotion results
- indirect factors (e.g. staff turnover).

chapter

11

Personal effectiveness and communication

In this chapter

- Personal development plan (PDP).
- Competence frameworks.
- Coaching, mentoring and counselling.
- Effective time management.
- Conflict.
- Communication process.

Exam focus

- Think of your personal development goals and how you would go about achieving them.
- Be aware of how coaching, counselling and training can help individuals develop.
- You need to understand how communication can be made effective.

Personal development plan (PDP)

Definition

A personal development plan is an action plan that incorporates a wide set of development opportunities.

Stages of PDP:

1 Analysing the current situation.
   - Identifying personal strengths and weaknesses.
   - Assessing future skill requirements.
   - Selecting areas for development.

2 Setting goals.
   - Examine reasons why certain tasks are not performed well.
   - Make sure that expectations are realistic.

3 Draw up an action plan.
   - Assess the methods available to address skills gap.
   - Gain formal commitment.
   - Set criteria for measuring progress.

4 Implement – often the hardest part.

Competence frameworks

Competences are the critical skills, knowledge and attitudes that a job-holder must have to perform effectively.

Competency frameworks attempt to identify all the competencies that are required by anyone taking on a particular role within an organisation. This can be used as a benchmark to either ensure that the correct individual is chosen for the role or as a way of checking that an existing member of staff has all the up to date skills required for their role.

Most competency frameworks cover the following categories:

- Communication skills.
- People management.
- Team skills.
- Customer service skills.

Coaching, mentoring and counselling

Definition

Coaching – trainee is put under the guidance of a more experienced member of staff.

Mentoring – more senior employee supports and guides the trainees through personal and career development.

Counselling – helping people to help themselves.

Features of coaching.

- Focused on task-specific objectives.
- Delivered in the work environment on one-to-one basis.
- Involves building up both skills and confidence.
- Coach is normally an expert on the topic in question.

Purposes of mentoring.

- Career function: gives exposure to higher level duties, provides opportunities and support when dealing with problems.
- Psychological function: creates a sense of acceptance and belonging, provides a role model.

Counselling deals with:

- problems arising within individual (e.g. frustration, lack of job satisfaction)
- problems caused by the organisation (e.g. overworking, uncertain future)
- external causes of problems (e.g. money, relationships, family).

Skills of a counsellor.

- Observant.
- Sensitive.
- Empathetic.
- Impartial.
- Discreet.

Effective time management

Good time management will allow the individual to:

- make the best use of available time
- reduce excessive workload
- prioritise important issues
- meet deadlines.

Time management techniques:

- planning and organising (e.g. schedules)
- keeping an activity log
- making lists and writing reminders
- being proactive and pre-empting issues
- deploying technology (e.g. calendar in Outlook).

Barriers to effective time management	**Ways to overcome the barriers**
Frequent interruptions Unpredictable nature of the job Having to travel long distances Bureaucratic procedures Putting things off	Be assertive, insist on more "personal space" Distinguish between urgent and important Multi-task, what could be done on the go? Focus on effectiveness Promise yourself a reward on completion

Conflict

Definition

Any personal divergence of interests between groups and individuals.

Types of conflict:

- **Vertical** – between individuals and groups at different levels of the organisation (e.g. between manager and junior).
- **Horizontal** – between individuals and groups at the same level of the organisation (e.g. between managers).

Conflict management strategies:

- **Denial** – ignore the conflict and hope that it resolves itself. Mainly used for minor conflicts.
- **Suppression** – threaten the conflicting parties with punishments if the conflict is not resolved. Short-term solution only.
- **Reduction** – manager acts as neutral third party and negotiates a compromise.
- **Resolution** – manager finds root cause of conflict and solves. Often time consuming and complex.

Communication process

Communication flows:

- downwards – manager to subordinate (e.g. orders, instructions, policies)
- upwards – subordinate to manager (e.g. feedback, performance results)
- horizontally – interdepartmental coordination (e.g. multi-disciplinary teams).

Barriers to effective communication	Ways to overcome the barriers
Different cultures and languages Noise and distortion Information overload Assumptions and prejudice Conflict between individuals	Provide training on cultural awareness Choose the most effective communication channel Prioritise and focus Be open-minded Rise above the differences

Communication patterns

Centralised: all communication goes through one person

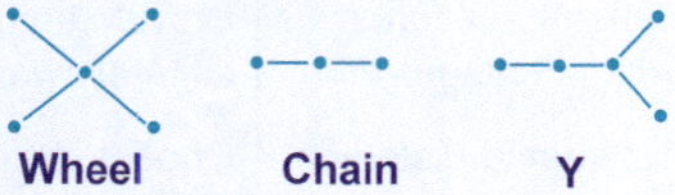

Decentralised: dispersed information processing

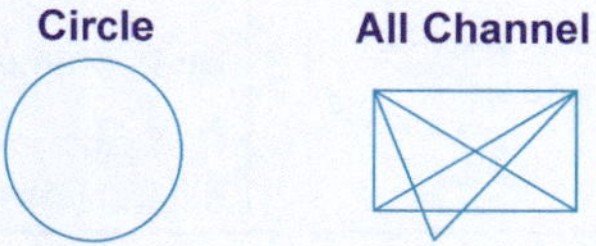

The wheel is the quickest system and the circle is the slowest.

The all channels system is best in complex situations, but under pressure all channels system restructures itself into a wheel.

Index

A

B

C

D

E

F

G

H

I

K

L

M